W9-CPG-965

Babies Nurse
Hardback ISBN 13: 978-1-930775-61-9 • ISBN 10: 1-930775-61-X | First Edition • October 2018
Paperback ISBN 13: 978-1-930775-71-8 • ISBN 10: 1-930775-71-7 | First Edition • October 2018
eBook eBook ISBN 13: 978-1-930775-36-7 • ISBN 10: 1-930775-36-9 | First Edition • October 2018
Part of the Platypus Media collection, Beginnings
Beginnings logo by Hannah Thelen, © 2018 Platypus Media

Written by Phoebe Fox
Watercolor Illustrations by Jim Fox
Line Drawings by Wesley Davies
Text and Watercolor Illustrations © 2018 Phoebe Fox
Line Drawings © 2018 Platypus Media, LLC

Project Manager: Ellen E. M. Roberts, Where Books Begin, Bethlehem, PA
Senior Editor: Anna Cohen, Washington, D.C.
Research Director: Don E. Wilson, Ph.D., Curator Emeritus, Smithsonian National Museum of Natural History, Washington, D.C.
Animal Research: Anna Cohen and Dia L. Michels, Washington, D.C.
Cover and Book Design: Holly Harper, Blue Bike Communications, Washington, D.C.
Basketball photograph on page 32, used with permission, Phoenix Suns

Also available in Bilingual (English/Spanish) • First Edition • June 2018
        Hardback ISBN 13: 978-1-930775-73-2 • ISBN 10: 1-930775-73-3
        Paperback ISBN 13: 978-1-930775-72-5 • ISBN 10: 1-930775-72-5
        eBook ISBN 13: 978-1-930775-40-4 • ISBN 10: 1-930775-40-7

Teacher's Guide available, in English and Spanish, at the Educational Resources page of PlatypusMedia.com.

Published by: Platypus Media, LLC
        725 8th Street, SE
        Washington, D.C. 20003
        202-546-1674 • Toll-free 1-877-PLATYPS (1-877-752-8977)
        Info@PlatypusMedia.com • www.PlatypusMedia.com

Distributed to the book trade by: National Book Network
        301-459-3366 • Toll-free: 1-800-787-6859
        CustServ@nbnbooks.com • www.NBNbooks.com

Library of Congress Control Number: 2018939430

10 9 8 7 6 5 4 3 2 1

The front cover may be reproduced freely, without modification, for review or non-commercial educational purposes.

All rights reserved. No part of this book may be reproduced in any form without the express permission
of the publisher. Front cover exempted (see above).

Printed in Canada.

Dear Reader,

We're excited to introduce you to this wonderful book about mammals, part of our Beginnings collection.

Scientific curiosity begins in childhood. Exposure to animals and their environments—whether in nature or in a book—is often at the root of a child's interest in science. Young Jane Goodall loved to observe the wildlife near her home, a passion that inspired her groundbreaking chimpanzee research. Charles Turner, pioneering entomologist, spent hours reading about ants and other insects in the pages of his father's books. Marine biologist, author, and conservationist Rachel Carson began writing stories about squirrels when she was eight. Spark curiosity in a child and watch them develop a lifelong enthusiasm for learning.

These beautifully illustrated, information-packed titles introduce youngsters to the fascinating world of animals, and, by extension, to themselves. They encourage children to make real-world connections that sharpen their analytical skills and give them a head start in STEM (science, technology, engineering, and math). Reading these titles together inspires children to think about how each species matures, what they need to survive, and what their communities look like—whether pride, flock, or family.

More than a simple scientific introduction, these animal stories illustrate and explore caring love across the mammal class. Showing children this type of attachment in the natural world fosters empathy, kindness, and compassion in both their interpersonal and interspecies interactions.

An easy choice for the home, library, or classroom, our Beginnings collection has something to spark or sustain budding curiosity in any child.

Enjoy!

Dia

Dia L. Michels
Publisher, Platypus Media

P.S. Our supplemental learning materials enable adults to support young readers in their quest for knowledge. Check them out, free of charge, at PlatypusMedia.com.

Babies Nurse

By Phoebe Fox
Illustrations by Jim Fox
Line drawings by Wesley Davies

DISCARD
STAUNTON PUBLIC LIBRARY

Platypus Media
Washington, D.C.

Filly nurses
in fresh air,
drinking milk
from mama mare.

Tigers nurse
for all they need,
nosing mama
while they feed.

Monkey nurses on a limb,
mother's arms protecting him.

Seal pup nurses on the beach,
mama stays within her reach.

Zebra nurses
in soft light,
under stripes
of black and white.

Puppies nurse, a golden heap,
snuggled up, they fall asleep.

Panda nurses on the ground,
mother's warmth and love abound.

Bat pup nurses at first light,
latched to mama, holding tight.

Polar cubs nurse in the snow,
mother's milk will help them grow.

Kittens nurse and gently purr,
nestled in their mama's fur.

Deer fawn nurses, unafraid,
mother's watchful in the glade.

Dolphin nurses
in the sea,
guarded by
her family.

Baby nurses
heart-to-heart,
mother's gift,
a natural art.

Answers to breastfeeding questions and breastfeeding support
can be found by visiting the following websites:

Breastfeeding USA
www.breastfeedingusa.org

The World Health Organization
www.who.int/topics/breastfeeding

International Lactation Consultant Association
www.ilca.org

The Lactation Institute
www.lactationinstitute.org

La Leche League International
www.llli.org

A portion of all sales of this book will be donated to La Leche League International.

For my mother and my three
nurslings –PF

For Aidan, Jamison, Caleb, Josie,
and Asher –JF

A cherished photo of
the author's mother
nursing her at St. Joseph's
Hospital in Phoenix
shortly after her birth.

Did You Know?

HORSE BABIES: FOALS

- Horses are *follow mammals*, meaning the young walk soon after birth and follow mom wherever she goes, feeding when they can.

- Foals nurse for three to four months before switching to solid food. Adult horses eat about 16 pounds of hay each day.

- Horses use their mouths only for eating. They breathe through their nostrils, not their mouth. Horses can't vomit or burp.

- Horses gallop at about 27 miles per hour (44 kph). When galloping, all four legs come off the ground at the same time.

TIGER BABIES: CUBS

- Tiger moms usually have three to four cubs in a litter. Cubs drink only mother's milk for their first six to eight weeks and then begin to eat solid food. After six months they learn how to hunt by following mom.

- Tigers are the largest members of the cat family. Unlike their smaller cousins, tigers cannot purr. Instead, big cats roar. No cat can do both.

- All tigers have a unique stripe pattern that helps others identify them. These stripes aren't just on their fur—their skin is striped, too.

- Tigers are excellent climbers, but their long, curved claws can't support their weight on their way down, forcing them to crawl backwards or jump.

MONKEY BABIES: INFANTS

- There are over 250 species of monkeys. They live on every continent except Australia and Antarctica. Different species vary in size, diet, and habits.

- The smallest monkey is the pygmy marmoset, which is only 5 inches (12 cm), about the size of a can of soda. The largest is the mandrill, which can grow to over 3 feet (1 meter).

- Monkeys are very social. They hold hands and groom one another, which helps build relationships and reinforce social structures in their community, or "troop."

- "New World" monkeys, who live mostly in trees, have *prehensile* tails which they can use to hold and grasp objects like a third hand.

SEAL BABIES: PUPS

- Seals are semi-aquatic marine mammals, meaning they spend most of their life in water, coming ashore to mate, give birth, breastfeed, molt, and escape predators.

- Pups wean abruptly when their mother returns to the water, leaving them on land to fend for themselves.

- Seals can hold their breath longer than any other mammal. They can even sleep underwater. They do this by resting half their brain at a time.

- The Caspian seal is the smallest species, about the size of an adult human—110 to 190 pounds (86 kg). The Elephant seal, the world's largest, can weigh up to 8,800 pounds (3,991 kg).

ZEBRA BABIES: FOALS

- Zebras live in herds for companionship and protection, but a mare will separate from the herd so she can be alone to give birth to her foal.

- Zebras are born with their unique stripe pattern, but at birth their stripes are brown instead of black.

- Within the first hour of life, zebra foals are able to stand up, walk, and even run.

- Foals recognize their mother by her distinctive scent, call, and the striped pattern on her rump and tail.

DOG BABIES: WHELPS/PUPPIES

- Dogs generally begin labor before dawn, but can take up to 20 hours to birth the entire litter. As labor continues, the firstborns begin to nurse.

- An average litter consists of five to six whelps, though this number varies widely by breed. Weaning occurs naturally around seven weeks of age.

- Humans rely primarily on their vision, but dogs rely on their sense of smell—and wet noses are better at smelling than dry ones.

- Humans keep dogs for companionship, but many dogs also work. Dogs herd farm animals, assist police, help the blind, and more.

PANDA BEAR BABIES: CUBS

- Panda cubs are among the smallest baby mammals—newborns are only about the size of a stick of butter. It takes two years to grow to an adult weight of 330 lbs (150 kg).

- Like human toddlers learning to walk, panda cubs are very clumsy. A cub will trip, roll, fall, and stumble as it explores its environment.

- Panda cubs start eating bamboo at around six months old, but mother's milk remains the main source of nutrition for the first year of life.

- It takes a panda only about 40 seconds to peel and eat a shoot of bamboo. Their throats have a protective lining that protects them from splinters.

BAT BABIES: PUPS

- Some bat species fight gravity and give birth upside-down. Others hang right-side-up to give birth, catching the pup in her tail membrane, the layer of thin skin between her legs.

- Pups feed from nipples located under their mother's wing. Some bats also have a second set of "pubic teats" lower down the abdomen that pups hold onto during flight.

- While some mammals can glide, bats are the only ones who actually fly. Their wings are similar to human hands, with membrane stretched over long fingers.

- Unlike birds and other flying animals, most bats can't take off from the ground. Instead, they have to drop from height to fly.

POLAR BEAR BABIES: CUBS

- Mother polar bears make dens in the snow where they give birth and care for their newborns. The den traps body heat, keeping the bear family warm.

- While in their winter den, mama bears don't eat, drink, or defecate for up to six months. Female polar bears are some of the longest-fasting mammals.

- Polar bears' black skin that absorbs sunlight, thick fur, and fat help keep them warm in freezing temperatures.

- Polar bears are the largest species of bear on Earth, and, at nearly 10 feet (3 meters) and 1,500 pounds (680 kg), are the world's largest land carnivore.

CAT BABIES: KITTENS

- Cats usually have a litter of three to five kittens, which are born blind and deaf. They begin to wean around four weeks of age.

- Most cats sleep 12 to 16 hours a day—by the time a cat is nine years old, it will have been awake for only three years of its life.

- All cats, from the cutest house cat to the wildest tiger, must eat meat to survive.

- Each cat has a unique pattern of bumps and ridges on their nose. Like human fingerprints, no two cats have identical nose-prints.

DEER BABIES: FAWNS

- Mother deer keep their fawns hidden in a safe place in the woods and return to nurse them every few hours.

- Deer milk is very high in protein and fat, which sustains the young for the long periods of time they must wait between feedings.

- Fawns have no distinctive smell, which helps hide them from predators. A mother deer will even eat her fawn's droppings to further conceal her baby.

- Deer are the only group of animals with velvet-covered bones, called antlers, on their heads. Every year, these antlers fall out, but soon a new set regrows.

DOLPHIN BABIES: CALVES

- Dolphins and other whales are the only mammals that are birthed tail-first. This prevents the calves from drowning during birth.

- Calves nurse for only five to ten seconds at a time, day and night. They need to swim to the surface to breathe air between squirts of breastmilk.

- Dolphins are incredibly social. They live, hunt, and play together in groups called pods. "Nanny" dolphins even help mothers birth and tend to the young.

- Dolphins have been known to stop and help injured strangers—including other dolphins, whales, and even humans.

HUMAN BABIES: INFANTS

- Human babies are the least mature of all mammals at birth and can do very little compared to other newborns. They know how to sleep, make their way to the breast, suck, and cry. They need the warmth of mom's body and are meant to be carried or held almost constantly. Carrying a child close to the body helps ease their transition to the outside world.

- Human babies need to breastfeed very often. A baby human's stomach is about the size of its fist. It is normal for a full-term baby to breastfeed eight to ten times every 24 hours. Small babies need to breastfeed even more frequently.

- During the first two years after birth, a human brain almost doubles in size. To fuel this growth, babies need a constant supply of nutrients. Thankfully, mother's milk is filled with these.

- What's at the end of your arm? For mammals, the options are wings, hooves, paws, flippers, or hands. Having hands gives us the ability to mold, hold, and shape our environment. We can pick up things and make tools. Our four fingers and opposable thumbs allow us to do much more complicated things than almost all other animals.

- Humans are the only land mammal that can be found on every continent on Earth, from the scorching heat of the Sahara Desert to the freezing temperatures of Antarctica. The only other animals that can be found on all seven continents are marine mammals (such as blue whales) who swim from place to place, birds who fly across oceans, and cockroaches.

BONUS: PETS

- Humans surround themselves with a variety of animals. Many serve a specific purpose: cows make milk, horses provide transportation, and sheep provide wool. Non-human animals have similar close relationships with one another (for example, birds pick off and eat pesky parasites from zebras), but humans also keep animals for companionship. We are the only creatures who keep pets.

- Pets actually help us in a number of ways. Pet owners are healthier, get more exercise, experience less stress and anxiety, and are more socially connected. Plus, early exposure to pets helps reduce the development of allergies and asthma. Pets help us grow a strong immune system, build emotional bonds, and develop empathy.

For more animal facts and fun hands-on activities, download the free Teacher's Guide at PlatypusMedia.com.

About the Author and the Illustrator

Phoebe Fox

Elementary school librarian, children's book author, and mother of three, **Phoebe Fox** wrote *Babies Nurse • Así se alimentan los bebés* to show children that all mammals provide milk for their babies. Phoebe sought to emphasize the warmth and beauty of nursing while demonstrating that all mammals share certain approaches to feeding, protecting, and teaching their young. Drawing on her own experiences as a breastfeeding mother, and wanting to present clear and accurate information about this "natural art," she consulted zoologists and pediatricians to put together this deceptively simple introduction. She is also the author of *Starry's Haircut, Starry Gets Lost,* and *Up Up Up* (winner of the 2015 First Edition Children's Book Contest). Phoebe lives in Phoenix, Arizona, with her husband and their three sons. She can be reached at PFox@PlatypusMedia.com.

When it came time to find an illustrator for the book, Phoebe asked her father-in-law, **Jim Fox**, if he would accept the task. Retired from the NBA, where he played for the Phoenix Suns, Jim was himself a recipient of plenty of his own mother's milk and says the benefits are obvious: he is 6' 10", healthy, and has produced wonderful kids and grandkids. The grandfather of five believes that nursing is a child's best start in life. Jim lives in Phoenix with his wife, Mary Alice. He can be reached at JFox@PlatypusMedia.com.

Jim Fox paints in his studio.

Jim Fox, ca. 1968

Phoebe Fox reads during a school visit.